THIS BOOK BELONGS TO

_____

FOR THE KIDS WHO WANT TO WIN

ISBN: 9798894582139

CAPTAIN SPLASH STOOD AT THE HELM OF HER SHIP, THE WAVE DANCER. "THE TREASURE OF MERMAID LAGOON AWAITS!" SHE SHOUTED TO HER CREW.

HER CREW CHEERED. "AYE, CAPTAIN SPLASH!" THEY CALLED BACK. SEAGULLS CIRCLED ABOVE, AND WAVES SPARKLED LIKE DIAMONDS IN THE SUNLIGHT.

THE MAP IN SPLASH'S HANDS SHOWED A TRAIL OF STARS LEADING TO MERMAID LAGOON. "FOLLOW THE STARS," SHE WHISPERED WITH EXCITEMENT.

SUDDENLY, THE SHIP JOLTED. "WHAT WAS THAT?" SPLASH ASKED. A DOLPHIN LEAPT OUT OF THE WATER, SQUEAKING HAPPILY.

"AHOY THERE!" SPLASH CALLED TO THE DOLPHIN. "DO YOU KNOW THE WAY TO MERMAID LAGOON?" THE DOLPHIN NODDED AND DOVE AHEAD.

THE WAVE DANCER FOLLOWED THE PLAYFUL DOLPHIN. THE CREW LEANED OVER THE RAILS, WATCHING ITS GRACEFUL FLIPS.

AS THE SUN SET, THE DOLPHIN SLOWED. IN THE DISTANCE, GLOWING WATER SHIMMERED LIKE LIQUID MOONLIGHT. "THAT MUST BE MERMAID LAGOON!" SPLASH EXCLAIMED.

THE LAGOON WAS SURROUNDED BY TALL, ROCKY CLIFFS. THE WATER GLOWED
SOFTLY, AND THE AIR FELT MAGICAL.

SPLASH DROPPED ANCHOR. "WE'LL NEED TO EXPLORE CAREFULLY," SHE
SAID. THE CREW LOWERED A SMALL ROWBOAT INTO THE GLOWING WATER.

JUST AS THEY PADDLED CLOSER TO THE LAGOON, A MELODIOUS VOICE FILLED THE AIR. "WHO DARES ENTER MERMAID LAGOON?" IT SANG.

A BEAUTIFUL MERMAID EMERGED, HER TAIL SHIMMERING WITH ALL THE COLORS OF THE SEA. "I AM CORAL," SHE SAID. "WHY HAVE YOU COME?"

SPLASH STOOD TALL. "WE SEEK THE TREASURE HIDDEN HERE," SHE
SAID. "WILL YOU HELP US?"

CORAL TILTED HER HEAD. "THE TREASURE IS PROTECTED BY MAGIC. ONLY THOSE WITH KIND HEARTS MAY FIND IT."

SPLASH SMILED. "WE MEAN NO HARM. WE ONLY WISH TO LEARN ITS SECRET." CORAL NODDED SLOWLY.

"FOLLOW ME," CORAL SAID. SHE DOVE BENEATH THE WAVES. SPLASH AND HER CREW HESITATED BUT JUMPED IN AFTER HER.

THE GLOWING WATER LIT THEIR WAY AS THEY SWAM DEEPER. FISH SWIRLED AROUND THEM, CREATING A SPARKLING UNDERWATER DANCE.

CORAL LED THEM TO A CAVE ENTRANCE. "THE TREASURE LIES WITHIN," SHE SAID. "BUT BEWARE—ONLY COURAGE AND KINDNESS WILL GUIDE YOU."

SPLASH TURNED TO HER CREW. "STAY CLOSE," SHE SAID. "AND REMEMBER CORAL'S WORDS."

INSIDE THE CAVE, GLOWING CRYSTALS LIT THE WALLS. THE CREW MARVELED AT THE BEAUTY AS THEY SWAM FORWARD.

SUDDENLY, A SHADOW MOVED. A GIANT OCTOPUS BLOCKED THEIR PATH, ITS TENTACLES WAVING MENACINGLY.

SPLASH HELD UP HER HANDS. "WE MEAN NO HARM," SHE SAID. "WE ONLY SEEK THE TREASURE OF KINDNESS."

THE OCTOPUS PAUSED, THEN SLOWLY MOVED ASIDE. "GO ON," IT SAID IN A DEEP VOICE. "YOU HAVE PASSED THE FIRST TEST."

THE CREW SWAM DEEPER INTO THE CAVE. "WHAT'S NEXT?" WHISPERED ONE OF
THEM. SPLASH KEPT HER EYES FORWARD.

THEY ENTERED A ROOM FILLED WITH SHIMMERING BUBBLES. EACH BUBBLE
HELD A GLOWING LIGHT. CORAL APPEARED BESIDE THEM AGAIN.

"CHOOSE WISELY," CORAL SAID. "ONLY ONE BUBBLE WILL REVEAL THE TREASURE."

SPLASH STUDIED THE BUBBLES. "IT'S NOT ABOUT RICHES," SHE SAID. "IT'S ABOUT WHAT'S INSIDE OUR HEARTS."

SHE REACHED FOR THE SMALLEST BUBBLE, GLOWING FAINTLY. AS SHE
TOUCHED IT, IT EXPANDED AND REVEALED A GOLDEN HEART.

"YOU HAVE CHOSEN WELL," CORAL SAID. "THE TREASURE IS KINDNESS, SHARED FREELY LIKE THE OCEAN'S WAVES."

THE GOLDEN HEART GLOWED BRIGHTER. SUDDENLY, THE CAVE FILLED WITH LIGHT. THE CREW CHEERED, THEIR HEARTS WARM.

"THANK YOU, CORAL," SPLASH SAID. "WE WILL CARRY THIS TREASURE WITH US WHEREVER WE GO."

CORAL SMILED. "REMEMBER, TRUE TREASURE ISN'T GOLD—IT'S HOW YOU TREAT OTHERS." SHE SWAM AWAY INTO THE GLOWING WATER.

BACK ON THE WAVE DANCER, SPLASH HELD THE GOLDEN HEART HIGH. "THIS IS A TREASURE WORTH SHARING!" SHE SAID.

THE CREW CHEERED. "CAPTAIN SPLASH! THE KINDEST PIRATE OF THE SEAS!"

AS THEY SAILED AWAY FROM MERMAID LAGOON, THE WATER SPARKLED
BRIGHTLY, AS IF WAVING GOODBYE.

SPLASH STOOD AT THE HELM, HER HEART FULL. "TO NEW ADVENTURES!" SHE CALLED. THE CREW CHEERED AGAIN.

THE DOLPHIN REAPPEARED, LEAPING JOYFULLY BESIDE THE SHIP. SPLASH LAUGHED. "GOODBYE, FRIEND! UNTIL WE MEET AGAIN."

THE WAVE DANCER SAILED INTO THE HORIZON, ITS SAILS BILLOWING
IN THE WIND, CARRYING ITS CREW TO NEW HORIZONS.

THE GOLDEN HEART HUNG IN THE CAPTAIN'S QUARTERS, A REMINDER OF THEIR MAGICAL ADVENTURE.

AND EVERY NIGHT, SPLASH TOLD HER CREW STORIES OF KINDNESS AND COURAGE, INSPIRING THEM TO LIVE WITH FULL HEARTS.

FOR CAPTAIN SPLASH AND HER CREW, THE REAL TREASURE WAS NOT GOLD BUT THE FRIENDS AND ADVENTURES THEY SHARED. THE END.

www.ingramcontent.com/pod-product-compliance
Lightning Source LLC
LaVergne TN
LVHW081702050326

832903LV00026B/1867